Table of Contents

S0-CVB-319

Career Launch Method:

What our partners are saying...

"Students have really enjoyed the action-oriented aspect of the program and feeling like they have **support in taking their career development to the next level.** You have helped my students feel much more confident in their abilities. I would highly recommend this program."

Tori Bussey-Neal
Student Success Coach
University of California, San Diego

"Career Launch's multi-modal programming has been an instrumental program to our students. **Many of them have landed jobs in the field of their choice and others have been able to enter a graduate program.** I am so happy to have the Career Launch program available to our students because I see how their confidence levels have increased."

Amanda Romero
Career Education Counselor/Professor
Counseling Department Chair
Irvine Valley College

What students are saying...

"I've never been afraid to act in my life, but I need to understand what I am doing. **This program has given me a system to act upon.** I have a career conversation scheduled for next week."

Mateo C.
Sophomore
Finance

"I really appreciate how structured the program is! The workbook does a great job of guiding me since I'm a visual and hands-on learner. I **like how there are direct and practical steps** that simplify previously unclear concepts. I wish I could have gone through the Career Launch program much sooner."

Kayla K.
Fourth-year
Psychology

About the Authors: Sean O'Keefe

I attended a community college, transferred to a 4-year state university, and am now an award-winning professor at a Jesuit university. I am the first person on my mom's side of the family to get a certificate or college degree, and my dad was the first person on his side of the family to go to a four-year college, after he transferred from a community college.

During undergrad, I earned three highly sought-after internships with the San Francisco 49ers, Oakland A's, and San Francisco Giants—and then a full-time job with the Oakland A's— **without having any connections nor the best resume or grades.** Only one of the three internships was posted online.

I later realized that while landing these positions, I had created the Career Launch Method. I was lucky to have received life-changing advice from my college professor Al Ferrer and my work supervisor Stephen Torres. Later, during grad school, professor Barry Posner recommended I start teaching the methodology to students. I'll be forever grateful to these mentors and to the many other professionals that helped me in my career journey.

After seven years with the Oakland A's and during my seven years as the vice president at a regional technology company, I started teaching at Santa Clara University to pay it forward in 2010. In 2018, with the encouragement of my university, colleagues, and former students, **Career Launch** was founded. In 2019, Santa Clara University provided financial support for us to scale our impact nationwide.

"A meaningful life should not be measured by your possessions or followers; it should be measured by personal growth and service to others.

Life is not about what you have, it's about what you do with what you have."

-Unknown

About the Authors: Marieli Rubio

As a first-generation Latina college student, I entered college without any professional contacts in my field of study, civil engineering. As a result, I struggled to know whether my interests were compatible with my technical career path. I knew I had to create a network from scratch to find mentors and internship opportunities but lacked a sense of direction.

After completing the **Career Launch** program my sophomore year of college, I applied my newly acquired skill set to reach out to professionals to have conversations about career paths and career options.

I built many professional relationships following the Career Launch Method, and landed a paid internship as a field engineer at a construction company the summer after my sophomore year.

It was a life-changing experience, allowing me to transfer what I had learned in the classroom to the field itself and increasing my self-confidence for my career search moving forward.

In 2020, I worked as a Partnerships Coordinator with Career Launch, where I realized that I was passionate about empowering students to be proactive and overcome barriers to professional development.

Intentional networking is a skill that can be learned, even if you consider yourself an introvert. It is so important to be **proactive** and **develop the skill of relationship-building early on.** I'm excited for you to embark on the step-by-step Career Launch program that teaches you the tips and tricks of connecting with professionals.

Trust me, despite any fears or concerns, following this method will pay off in the long run.

"Choose a job you love, and you will never have to work a day in your life."

\- Confucius

Why Is Completing This Workbook Important?

Being a student is a time to learn about yourself and about what careers might interest you in the future. It's completely fine and normal if you aren't sure what career you want to pursue. Your interests will likely change over time, and you may work dozens of different jobs throughout your life. The reality is that:

The average person spends **90,000 hours** at work over their lifetime* $= \dfrac{1}{3}$ of your life is spent at work

* Source: Susan Peppercorn, "Why You Should Stop Trying to Be Happy at Work," Harvard Business Review, July 26, 2019.

Explore Majors, Programs of Study, & Careers

Create Strategic Social Capital with Alumni

Land Internships & Jobs in the Hidden Job Market

Develop Internal Advocates with Employers of Interest

What is the Career Launch Method?

This workbook will show you how to proactively set up meetings with professionals—which we call **career conversations**—that will help you build relationships, explore career options and land the jobs and internships you want.

It's likely that one of the main reasons you decided to attend college was to earn a high-quality job afterward. But landing internships and jobs can be difficult, and it can be even tougher to land the ones you really want. **Only 20% of jobs and internships are posted online.**[1] Your odds of landing an interview were **less than 2%**[2] before the COVID-19 pandemic, and are even lower now.

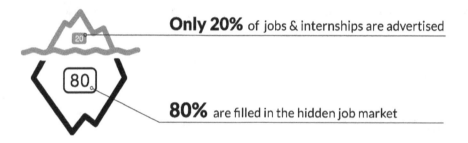

Only 20% of jobs & internships are advertised

80% are filled in the hidden job market

How can you access the 80% of jobs in the hidden job market? How can you stand out from the crowd?

In this workbook, we'll cover the essential steps to launching your career. The **8-step Career Launch Method** is a proven framework that has worked for thousands of students across the country.

The Career Launch Method isn't just about getting a job and increasing your social capital. **You'll gain the tools to step out of your comfort zone, overcome any emotional or psychological barriers to strategic, intentional networking, and increase proficiency in the NACE 8 Career Readiness Competencies** in the process.

1. Bill Burnett and Dave Evans, Designing Your Life, 2018.   2. Rebecca Bosl, "Applying Online? How to Improve Your Odds of Landing the Interview," Forbes, 2019.

How This Workbook Will Help You

 Explore Majors, Programs of Study, and Career Options

Being a student is the time to be proactive about your future career. Conducting career conversations with professionals and employers of interest will help you discover which jobs, industries, and career paths might interest you, as well as help you build self-confidence.

 Develop Internal Advocates and Land Internships and Jobs

Research shows that students who conduct career conversations are **four times more likely** to land internships during college than students who don't. Career conversations are proven to be a highly-effective strategy for getting your foot in the door and increasing your chances of landing a full-time job that you really want. This is because the best way to land internships and jobs is to know employees at the organizations where you want to work.

Additionally, research shows that job applicants who get a referral from a current employee are **12 times more likely** to be hired than applicants who only apply online.[3] This workbook will show you how to create and sustain relationships with professionals who can be internal advocates and give you access to the hidden job market.

> **Don't take any shortcuts. Be sure to follow all the steps and micro-steps of the Career Launch Method to maximize your success.**

3. Brown, Setren, and Topa, Do Informal Referrals Lead to Better Matches?, IZA Discussion Paper no. 8175, May 2018.

"Sometimes, you have to look back in order to understand the things that lie ahead."

Yvonne Woon

"The Career Launch techniques allowed me to set up career conversations with multiple professionals in my area of interest. Several of my meetings resulted in introductions, mentorship, valuable advice, and even internship offers. **I have been able to choose between dream internships multiple times.** I will undoubtedly continue to practice these teachings as my career progresses."

Anjali R.
Class of 2021

Discernment: Explore Career Options & Prioritize the Organizations You Want to Work For

Launching Your Career

The first step to launching your career isn't to look at what opportunities are available in the world and posted online, it's to **look inside yourself** at your interests, skills, and character traits.

Your interests and skills will likely be found through experimentation as you gain experience and knowledge in the classroom and the workplace. The Career Launch Method will **accelerate your career exploration and readiness, increase your social capital by strategically creating relationships with professionals (internal advocates), and provide you access to the hidden job and internship market.**

Don't Overthink This Step

Step 1 asks you to **identify 10 organizations** you might want to work for. Don't spend too long on this activity. The key to the Career Launch Method is **taking action**, which **can't happen if you over analyze** the many possibilities that exist for your career.

Your goals are to answer the questions on the following pages and write down as many organizations on your initial top ten list (p. 19) as you can in the next 30 minutes. If you don't finish your *initial* list, make time to do so in the next two or three days.

Remember that **discernment is an ongoing process**, and it's normal to make **changes** and **additions** to your list as you move forward.

Questions for Career Reflection

- What have been the most impactful events in your life?
- Who do you admire?
- What are you good at?
- What can you be paid for?
- What does the world need?
- What do you love to do?

Personal Reflection

▶ What comes to mind when you think about the tasks you enjoy doing?

_____

_____

_____

_____

▶ When you reflect on your life, what experiences have impacted you most?

_____

_____

_____

_____

▶ What skills or strengths do you currently have?

(If you've taken the CliftonStrengths assessment, the Meyers-Briggs Type Indicator, or another personality/strengths test, reference your results. Your school may also have resources to help you.)

_____

_____

_____

_____

> _Reminder: If these questions are challenging, reach out to a career counselor, trusted family member, friend, mentor, coach, or professor and chat about your skills, experiences, and future career._

Ikigai Activity - Jot your thoughts in the 4 boxes below

What do you love?

1) What have you never gotten bored of?
2) What's something you've always been drawn back to do over time?
3) What gets you in the flow?

What does the world need?

1) How can you contribute to make your community a better place?
2) What does your community or our country need more of? (i.e. Housing for the homeless, help with global warming and pollution, etc.)

What are you good at?

1) What skills have you been spending time on?
2) What do people look to you for help with?
3) What are some of the things you want to be good at?

What can you get paid for?

1) What have you been paid for before?
2) How important is money to you?
3) What type of businesses are thriving in your community?

* Source: Discover your Purpose in Life (Ikigai in 4 Steps). Mossery.

Discovering Your Ikigai

In Japan, there is a concept called *ikigai*, or *a reason for being*. Your ikigai is the **sense of purpose, meaning, and well-being** that arises from living a fulfilling life. For example, why do you get out of bed in the morning? Ikigai is your answer.

You may be thinking, *why do I need to figure out why I exist when all I want is an internship to gain some experience or a job to pay my bills?* **The point is to reflect on how your skills and interests align with what organizations value, what you can bring to this world, and how you can maximize fulfillment in your career.**

* *Vocation* refers to a career path that you feel particularly drawn toward or called to pursue.

10 Factors That Matter in a Job

1. Job Function
Will you be able to use your skills and interests in the job role? Will you find the work meaningful?

2. Learning/Growth Opportunities
Could you take on exciting projects? Are there advancement opportunities? Will the job help you build valuable skills?

3. Relationship with Supervisor
How closely will you work with your supervisor? Do you value that person as a leader and mentor?

4. Time Commitment
How many hours per week will you be working? Can you work remotely?

5. Organizational Culture and Values
How do employees describe the leadership, environment, values, mission and ethics of the company?

6. Organizational Size
Is this a corporation? A health clinic? A school district? A regional organization? A start-up? What environment are you best suited for?

7. Industry
Do you value the industry or business more than the job function you will be performing? Or, vice versa?

8. Geography/Remote Work
Where would you like to live? Would you like to work remote or hybrid? Are you willing to commute or relocate? Are you willing to travel frequently?

9. Risk/Security
What sort of job security does this job provide? Is the company in a stable financial position? A stable industry?

10. Compensation
How much will you be paid? Hourly or salary? What benefits will be provided, and which are most important to you?

Write down your thoughts on each job characteristic	Importance (1-100 Scale)
1. Job Function	
2. Learning/Growth Opportunities	
3. Relationship with Supervisor	
4. Time Commitment	
5. Organizational Culture and Values	
6. Organizational Size	
7. Industry	
8. Geography/Remote Work	
9. Risk/Security	
10. Compensation	

Choosing Your Top 10 Organizations

To learn about organizations and companies you can add to your top 10 list, go to *www.careerlaunch.academy/resources* and click on **Step 1: Discernment**. Then click, **"How to Identify..."**

Step 1: Login with the credentials provided   `Sign In`

Step 2: Click on "Employers by Major"   **Employers by Major**

Step 3: Select a Major/Program of Study to locate associated employers   **By Major**

Step 4: Find and Select the State you'd like to work   **By State**

Filter

Step 5: Use the "Filter" button to narrow down options based on city, zipcode, etc.   `Filter`

City

State   MA

Zipcode

Additional Resources for Discernment and Exploration:

1. Utilize **"What Can I Do With This Major?"** at *www.careerlaunch.academy/resources*

2. **Visit your school's career center website for career exploration resources. If your school has an alumni platform, explore the organizations represented there.**

3. Follow steps on page 24 of this workbook to access the **LinkedIn alumni tool.** You can enter a keyword like "design" or "engineer" in the search box.

4. **Search online** based on your interests. Example searches:

🔍 best healthcare companies in Nebraska   🔍 top companies to start a career in sales

My Top 10 Organizations

Companies, Non-Profits, Government Agencies, Social Enterprises, Startups, Local and Mid-Size businesses, Fortune 500 Companies

1. _____

2. _____

3. _____

4. _____

5. _____

👥 **73% of professionals work in a field unrelated to their major** (Washington Post) It's okay to add orgs that don't correlate to your major.

6. _____

7. _____

8. _____

9. _____

10. _____

Note: Your list will probably change later, and that's okay. Just focus on finishing this initial list within two or three days.

"Success at anything will always come down to this: focus and effort, and we control both."

— *Dwayne (The Rock) Johnson*

"In May of my junior year, I didn't have a summer internship, and I felt mildly panicked. Following the Career Launch Method, I found a local company on LinkedIn and emailed the Chief Marketing Officer to ask if he would be open to a conversation. He quickly responded, and from there things took off. **I landed a part-time internship, which led to a full-time job upon graduation.**"

Erin F.
Class of 2022

Strategic Research: Discover Professionals Who Can be Helpful to You

How to Target Professionals Who Can be Most Helpful to You

Try to identify some or all of the attributes below for the professionals you add to your Strategic Contacts Lists (p. 31-35).

1. Job Function

A job function describes a general category of job roles at an organization, such as finance, nurse, human resources, teacher, marketing, office assistant, design, etc. **Targeting professionals in the job function you are most interested in is a great way to discover insights about your job types of interest.**

2. Job Title

Hiring managers are supervisors or managers of other employees. These professionals are more likely to make hiring decisions than non-manager professionals. Unless you are trying to get a job in HR, **DO NOT target recruiters or HR personnel.** You want to target **mid-level management** professionals who are "Directors" or "Supervisors" in the departments or divisions of your organizations of interest. See the graphic on page 23.

3. Location

Identify people who are located at the office or worksite where you want to work. This is not important if you are looking for a remote position.

4. Shared interest or background *(optional)*

Your school's alumni are more likely to speak with you, even if they have never met you. Other things you may have in common that can establish a connection include **shared first-generation status; community college background; veteran/military background; ethnic heritage; hobby** (if discussed on the professional's LinkedIn, personal website, or biography page); involvement with a sport, community group, non-profit, etc.

Of your Top 10 organizations on page 19, **choose five to focus on**. Write them below and on the top of pages 31-35, your Strategic Contacts Lists.

1. _____

2. _____

3. _____

4. _____

5. _____

Your goal for Step 2 is to write down the names and contact information of at least **15 professionals who work in mid-level management positions**.

▶ What job functions and job titles would you like learn more about?

_____

_____

Executives
- Executive Director
- CEO,COO,CFO, Chief Executive _____
- President
- Vice President of _____

Mid-Level Management
- Director of _____
- Senior Manager of _____
- Supervisor

Entry-Level
- Representative
- Coordinator
- Assistant

3 Research Methods

1. Organization Websites and Social Media Profiles

Check the organization's website to see if it has employee biographies. Some organizations include information about current projects or open positions. An organization's LinkedIn, Facebook, and Twitter may share relevant links or feature certain employees and their work.

Even if you find enough professionals on LinkedIn, researching the organization is an important step before conducting a career conversation.

2. LinkedIn Alumni Tool

Go to *Linkedin.com/alumni* or search for your university in the search field and click *Alumni* in the sidebar.

You can add filters for an industry, company or location to find alumni who match these qualities.

> **Note:** *If you don't already have a LinkedIn account, navigate to www.linkedin.com to create a free account. For best practices on creating your LinkedIn profile, see page 41.*

3. LinkedIn Search & Filters

Use LinkedIn filters to find professionals in a certain company, role, or industry. Enter a company name or industry, then click a result that says "people."

a.

b.

To modify your search, click *All Filters*

c.

Add filters that are relevant to you, then click "apply."
You can always modify the search filters later and perform multiple searches for different companies and job functions.

> **Note:** *LinkedIn requires you to have a minimum of 30 connections to view all profiles without restrictions.*

How to Find Work Email Addresses

Over ten years of data shows that **email is the most effective way** to reach out to professionals. But how can you find the work email of a professional you don't know?

Begin by checking the company website. Then use the following tools until you find a working email address. *Note: none of the following resources are 100% accurate.* **Never email someone's non-work email unless it is listed publicly on their personal or organization website.**

Although you may need to enter your email to create an account for some of these services, you don't need to pay. If one of these services isn't working for you, try another. These are all ethical!

For a full list of email-finding tools, visit *www.careerlaunch.academy/resources* or scan the QR code to the right.

Try a Simple Online Search

Depending on industries, email addresses can be easily found by navigating through their website and searching for their directory.

🔍 Saint Helena Unified School District directory ←——— "Directory" or "Meet Our Team" are key words

Navigate to your College's Alumni Platform

If your school has an alumni platform (typically found through the Career Center or Alumni Center websites), you can use it to identify professionals interested in connecting with students.

Note: If you can't find the professional's email address or phone number using the 4 research methods, move on to another contact.

Apollo.io - LinkedIn Extension

1. Following the steps you followed to download Clearbit on the Chrome Webstore, search for Apollo.io and "Add as an Extension"

2. Open your LinkedIn profile. You should have this image on the right hand side →

3. Search a professional's profile, then click on the Apollo.io icon to find their information

Clearbit Connect - A Gmail Extension

1. Download the Clearbit Connect Chrome browser extension

2. Click the Clearbit button on the right sidebar in Gmail

3. Search for an organization

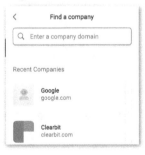

4. Search for a name, role or title

RocketReach.co

1. Go to www.rocketreach.co and create a free account

2. Search for names or organizations

Hunter.io

If you cannot find a professionals email address on their company's/ organization's website or by using Clearbit, Rocketreach, or Apollo, you might need to make an educated guess using **Hunter.io.**

Hunter.io will show you the most common pattern, or email syntax, for a specific company, such as **[first name] . [last name]@company.com**.

1. Go to www.hunter.io and create a free account

2. Enter in the name of your desired organization

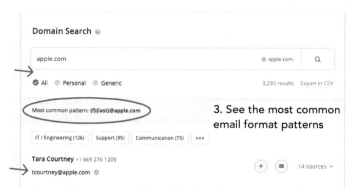

3. See the most common email format patterns

How to Find Organization Main Line Phone Numbers

Although phone calls may seem outdated to you, the reality is that they are still common in the professional world (especially for employees over the age of 40). Additionally, picking up the phone will help you stand out from a professional's crowded email inbox.

Most likely, you will need to find the organization's main office line and then speak to a receptionist or find the employee through an automated system. Don't call a professional's cell phone number unless they give it to you or it's publicly displayed on their organization's website.

Here are the steps to follow:

1. Check the organization's website

Many organizations post phone numbers for their different office locations online, but some only list one number on their Contact Us page. When you are searching, take note of the office location of the professional you are researching, and try to find the phone number for that office.

Some organizations have employee bio webpages which include the extension of the person. If this is the case, you're all set, but don't expect to find extensions for most employees.

"You must be willing to do the things today others won't do, in order to have the things tomorrow others won't have."

\- Les Brown

---

2. Search on Google

There's one important trick here: **search for both the organization's name and the city location.**

Look at the difference:

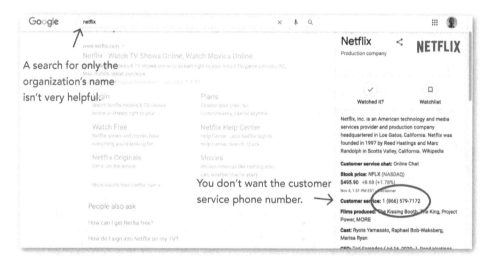

A search for only the organization's name isn't very helpful.

You don't want the customer service phone number. →

Instead, search: **[organization name] + [location] + "office"**

Correct search

This is the office phone number you want

For a digital version, visit careerlaunch.academy/resources

Strategic Contacts Lists

Organization #1: _____

Main Line
Phone #: _____

Office Mailing
Address: _____

Employee Name	Job Title	Work Email	Shared interest or background? Alumni?
Additional Contact:			
Additional Contact:			

Organization #2: _____

Main Line
Phone #: _____

Office Mailing
Address: _____

_____

Employee Name	Job Title	Work Email	Shared interest or background? Alumni?
Additional Contact:			
Additional Contact:			

Strategic Contacts Lists

Organization #3: _____

Main Line
Phone #: _____

Office Mailing
Address: _____

Employee Name	Job Title	Work Email	Shared interest or background? Alumni?
Additional Contact:			
Additional Contact:			

Organization #4: _____

Main Line
Phone #: _____

Office Mailing
Address: _____

Employee Name	Job Title	Work Email	Shared interest or background? Alumni?
Additional Contact:			
Additional Contact:			

Organization #5: _____

Main Line
Phone #: _____

Office Mailing
Address: _____

Employee Name	Job Title	Work Email	Shared interest or background? Alumni?
Additional Contact:			
Additional Contact:			

"Professional branding is the art of becoming knowable, likable and trustable."

John Jantsch

"I graduated high school with a 2.2 GPA. My father is a farmer and my mother works for a laundry company. No one in my family went to college. I started at a community college, but then was accepted to transfer to UC Berkeley, and I landed internships with Intel and General Motors. **The Career Launch Method gave me a system** to connect with hiring managers and to compete and succeed professionally."

Victor Z.
Class of 2022

Step 3

Professional Brand: Enhance Your Online

What is your professional brand?

The term "professional brand" refers to how people perceive you in professional settings based on your skills, professional experience, how you treat people, and other information about you. Your "online brand" is the story you tell about yourself through your application materials, social media, and any other mentions of you online.

When you reach out to a professional asking to speak with them, they will naturally want to know who you are. Their first step will likely be to look you up online to ensure that you are a real and genuine person. Professionals are likely to look at your LinkedIn profile to familiarize themselves with you.

Following the action items in this step will raise the odds that professionals say 'yes' to your requests for career conversations.

Whether or not professional branding and LinkedIn are new to you, you can find more resources and video tutorials on our website at _www.careerlaunch.academy/resources_ or by scanning the QR code on the right.

Essential vs. Non-Essential Actions

You should complete these two items before moving on to Step 4:

1. Email Signature
2. A basic LinkedIn profile (with a headshot, headline, and About, Experience and Education sections)

These elements of your professional brand are "nice-to-haves" but shouldn't prevent you from moving on to Step 4:

- An advanced LinkedIn profile (recommendations or media links)
- Portfolio (examples of your work in a Google Slides presentation, PDF, or personal website)

Professional Brand Reflection

▶ How do I want to be perceived by my peers/ professionals?

_____

_____

_____

_____

_____

▶ What past projects or work samples would you be proud to show a future employer?

_____

_____

_____

_____

_____

▶ What information about you is currently visible online? Google your name, and visit all your social media accounts besides LinkedIn. Should any of them be set to private?

_____

_____

_____

_____

Crafting an Email Signature

As you can imagine, many professionals will not say "Yes" the very first time they receive an email from you. To increase your chances of getting a response, make your email as professional and simple as possible.

An email signature bolsters your credibility because it gives the recipient relevant information about you. At the very least, include your **name, photo, major or program of study, your school, and a link to your LinkedIn profile**. If you have a personal website or online portfolio, you should include links to those as well. You may not be comfortable having your phone number on your email signature at all times. For the purpose of reaching out to professionals, **it increases transparency and the likeliness of you receiving a "Yes."**

To learn how to create an email signature, watch a tutorial, or use one of our templates, visit *www.careerlaunch.academy/resources*.

Here are several samples of excellent email signatures:

Sonia Gonzalez
Business Administration
San Diego City College
(123) 456-7890
www.linkedin.com/in/sonia-gonzalez12

Henry Gabriel
Penn State, Sociology
VP of Interact Club | (123) 456-7890
www.linkedin.com/in/henrygabriel1234
www.henrygabrielportfolio.com

Kirthi Ramjin
Art & Design, Games Playable Media
University of Iowa
LinkedIn: www.linkedin.com/in/kirthiramjin
(123) 456-7890

LinkedIn Essentials

Most professionals who receive an email from you will look you up before responding. If you are reaching out in a professional context, they will most likely look at your LinkedIn profile.

LinkedIn is the world's largest professional networking site, with 722+ million users and 50 million companies all over the world.

Creating a LinkedIn profile will help showcase your experience and skills to future employers and professionals you contact for career conversations. Here's how to get started:

1. Add a profile photo

A headshot makes your profile more credible and authentic. A picture from a phone camera is **works well**, but make sure it's not pixelated. Try to get a picture where your head takes up about half the frame. Your profile photo should be well-lit and have a relatively simple background.

Good Headshots:

Bad Headshots:

Blurry, black & white, smiling too much   Selfie   Too close

2. Edit your headline

A headline is automatically created based on your current position, but you may want to edit your headline. A generic headline like "Student at De Anza College" is okay, but you may want to include multiple phrases separated by the vertical dash character like this:

"Business Student at De Anza College | Aspiring Marketing Intern"

Try to think about what high-level overview of you would be accurate and eye-catching.

Sample profile header:

3. About section

This overview of yourself should be 1-3 paragraphs. You can tell a short backstory about what you are interested in and why. The final paragraph should say what you are currently looking for, such as "I am currently looking for a fall 2021 internship in finance. If you know of an open position or would like to chat, email me at _____."

Sample about section:

About

I am a second-year student at De Anza College studying business administration. A year ago, I spoke with a portfolio manager at BlackRock about the power of passive investing through ETFs, which sparked my interest in portfolio management.

In my first two years at De Anza College, I have furthered my understanding of business and investments through classwork and business simulations. I improve operations at De Anza's help desk by providing positive customer support.

I am currently looking for an internship in portfolio management. If you have a position opening or would like to talk about business, you can reach me at john.smith@example.com.

Summing up your professional identity, interests, and goals in just a few sentences can be tricky, so take some time to brainstorm ideas below. Keep it short and professional, but don't be afraid to talk about what you really care about. You can even mention any relevant and appropriate hobbies.

▶ Ideas for my About section:

_____

_____

_____

_____

_____

_____

_____

_____

_____

4. Experience

Your LinkedIn experience should highlight your relevant jobs, internships, unpaid work, and volunteer experiences. Fill out each section of the "add work experience" form on your LinkedIn profile. If the organization has a presence on LinkedIn, select it in the dropdown menu so that the logo shows up.

In the description section, tell how you have added value to that organization—similar to your resume, but in sentence or bullet-point form.

Sample experience entry:

Experience

Administrative Assistant
De Anza College
Sep 2019 – Present · 10 mos
Cupertino, California, United States

I provide the help desk at De Anza College with information regarding student and administrative inquires. Daily tasks include taking all college-directed phone calls, opening and closing the building, setting up and working special events, and promoting stellar customer service.

5. Education

Fill out the education section on LinkedIn and include any relevant details that could differentiate you such as a high GPA, leadership in a student organization or any honors or awards.

Sample education entry:

Education

De Anza College
Bachelor of Business Administration - BBA, Finance, General
2019 – 2021
Activities and Societies: Investing Club (VP Marketing), Band (member), Multicultural center (VP Marketing)

Advanced LinkedIn Tips

(Note: We don't want to stop you from moving on to Step 4 even if you have not completed the micro-steps).

1. Custom URL

Creating a custom URL based on your name can make it easy for recruiters and hiring managers to find you. Your custom URL should ideally be the same as your name, perhaps with a dash in the middle or a number at the end if necessary.

Once you create a custom URL, add it to your email signature and resume.

Follow the images below after navigating to your profile while logged in. This menu will likely appear in the top right corner.

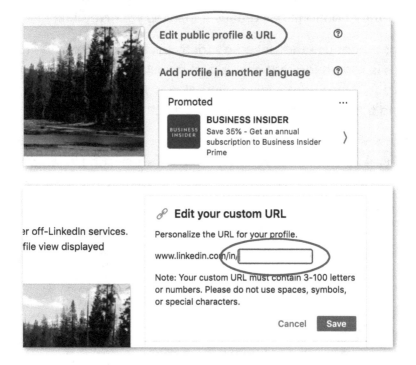

2. Add media

If there are any websites or articles that show the work you've done in any section (Summary, Work Experience or Education), you can link the website or upload an image or PDF.

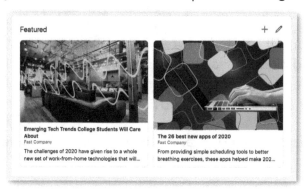

3. Ask for a Recommendation

Consider asking a former boss, coach, or professor for a recommendation. This greatly enhances your credibility.

Tip: do not use the LinkedIn tool to ask for a recommendation. This is something that should first be asked on the phone or in-person. Once you receive a verbal or written confirmation, then send the request from inside LinkedIn.

Note: if you have a paper letter of recommendation, we suggest you ask for the recommendation to be added on LinkedIn.

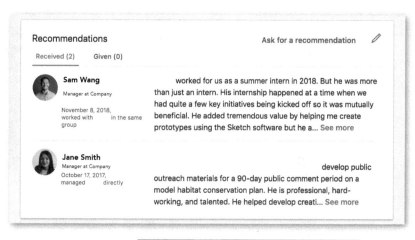

Career Launch Method | 1 | 2 | 3 | 4 | 5 | 6 | 7 | 8 |

LinkedIn Questions

▶ What words would you want someone to use to describe you after seeing your Linkedin profile?

_____

_____

_____

_____

▶ What is the strongest part of your profile?
Which sections might you need to keep editing later?

_____

_____

_____

▶ Identify 2-3 LinkedIn profiles that you admire and take notes on why you like them. What stands out to you?

_____

_____

_____

_____

_____

How to Create a Portfolio

(Do not let this micro-step stop you from moving on to Step 4)

Creating a portfolio will differentiate you and can provide a competitive advantage over other students when applying to any job or contacting a professional.

The goal of a portfolio is to show examples of your work as well as your process for solving professional problems. The projects you show could be school projects, volunteer experiences, minimum-wage service jobs, internships, personal projects, etc.

Depending on your goals, your portfolio could take many forms. A personal website or blog can be very effective, but take more time to create. Or, your school may have an online portfolio tool. Here, I'll show you how to **create a simple portfolio in Google Slides.**

1. Create a new Google Slides presentation.

2. Outline your slides. There's no one correct way to do this, but here's an example:

    1. Title slide with a headshot and brief summary of who you are
    2. Table of contents slide covering the 3 projects you'll cover
    3. Project #1: Part 1. Context, your actions, and results
    4. Project #1: Part 2. Photos, graphics, screenshots, diagrams, etc.
    5. Project #2: Part 1
    6. Project #2: Part 2
    7. Project #3: Part 1
    8. Project #3: Part 2
    9. Conclusion slide with your contact information and a sentence about what professional opportunities you're interested in

3. In a separate document, begin writing out each section. Collect or create visuals (screenshots, photos, graphics, charts) to show examples of your work. Then, start making your slides!

4. If possible, set the sharing settings to "anyone with a link can view." You may need to make a copy from a non-school Google account to access this setting. If you're having trouble, simply download your portfolio as a PDF.

Portfolio Examples

Anyone can make an excellent portfolio, no matter your experience or design skills. To see examples and templates, visit www.careerlaunch.academy/resources.

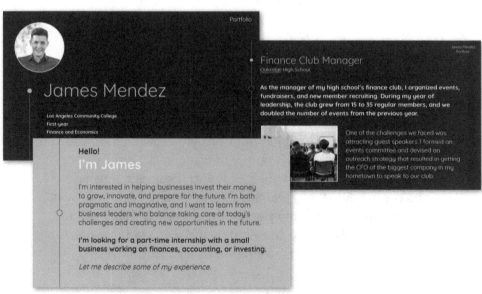

"Sometimes people are put off by networking as something tainted by flattery and the pursuit of selfish advantage. But virtue in obscurity is rewarded only in heaven. **To succeed in this world, you have to be known by people.**"

- Sonia Sotomayor

"I really wanted to work for a particular company, but didn't know how to stand out from the crowd. I followed the 10-Day Outreach Strategy and secured 10 in-person and 2 phone conversations. Building these relationships paid off. I eventually learned that **someone I had met was so impressed with my persistent outreach that I would automatically get to the final round.** I landed the internship! This method has had a tremendous impact on my life."

Henning J.
Class of 2021

Step 4

Outreach: How to Play the Student Card to Set up Career Conversations

The Student Card

We are giving you an assignment to conduct at least two career conversations. When you reach out to professionals, we highly encourage you to explicitly **state that you are a student and you have an assignment.** Professionals remember what it was like to be a student with no job and few connections.

Playing the student card will greatly increase the chances that a professional will want to help you. The Career Launch Method will show you how to be respectful of professionals' time and express gratitude with connections you have strong, weak, loose, or no ties.

Strong Ties vs Weak Ties vs Loose Ties vs No Ties

Strong Ties
People you know very well

Weak Ties
People who you interact less often or haven't seen in a long time

Loose Ties
People who you haven't met but likely could be introduced to by a strong or weak tie

No ties - no relationship at all

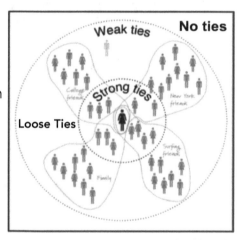

Howard Ogawa, 2012

In-person vs. Video Chat vs. Phone Call

In-person conversations are ideal because it is easiest to form a meaningful connection, and if these are scheduled at the professional's workplace, the conversation can lead to an office tour and you'll get the best sense of company culture.

Video chats are preferable to phone calls because seeing facial expressions makes it easier to form a deeper connection. Phone calls are better than nothing, but they should be your last resort.

Connecting with Strong, Weak, or Loose Ties

You can group people in your warm network into three categories. See below, along with templates that you can use to set up career conversations and boxes to write down names of people who come to mind.

Ask the following question to people in your warm network:

You don't happen to know anybody who works in [industry or specific job function], do you?

Even if they don't directly work in the industry you're interested in, it's possible that they will know someone who does.

1) People who you know and feel comfortable contacting

Template:

Hi _____,

I have an assignment this [semester/quarter/summer] to conduct two career conversations. Can we schedule 20 minutes to connect later this week or next week?

Thank you,
[your name]

▶ Uncles, Aunts, Cousins, Neighbors, Family, Friends, Co-Workers, Parent(s) Friends, Guardian(s) Friends

Make your list:

2) People you know but haven't talked to in a while and are unsure if you can/should reach out to them

Template:

Hi _____,

It's been a while, I hope you are doing well.
This is [(your name) from _____]. I have an assignment this [semester/quarter/summer] to conduct two career conversations. Can we schedule 20 minutes to connect later this week or next week?

Thank you for your consideration,
[your name]

Make your list:

3) People that your professors, friends, classmates, family know, but who you don't know personally

(We call these 2nd connections. See the micro-step below.)

Template:

Hi _____,

I have an assignment this [semester/quarter/summer] about career discernment. You are connected with [name of person] and I'd love for you to introduce me and/or provide me [his/her] email address. I would like to connect with [her/him] for my assignment. Would you be willing to assist me?

Thank you,
[your name]

▶ Second Connections (i.e. Classmate's parent, professor's friend, etc.)

Make your list:

Micro-step: Identify your 2nd Connections

There are two ways to identify 2nd connections:

1. Ask the people *you* know if *they* know anyone who works for any of your Top 10 organizations or in industries or job functions that interest you. Ask the "You don't happen to know..." question listed in bold on page 51.

2. Use LinkedIn filtering for each of your Top 10 organizations and select "2nd connections" from the filtering menu. Anyone who is listed as a 2nd connection knows someone who you are connected with. In this scenario, you can ask the person you know to make an introduction for you.

To view a video tutorial, visit

www.careerlaunch.academy/resources

> *"The best way to predict the future*
> *is to create it."*
>
> - Abraham Lincoln

Contacting someone you've been recommended to speak with
(but don't have an email introduction):

Example: You are speaking to John, and he recommends that you contact his colleague Sherry, but does not send an introduction email. In this case, **you** need to send the introduction email to Sherry. You will want to **strategically mention** that John referred you.

Here's a template for what you would send to Sherry in this case:

Subject Line: Referred by [John]

Dear [Sherry],

I'm a student at [UC San Diego] and I'm really interested about starting my career [in the journalism field.] I had a great conversation with [John] last week, and he recommended you as a great person to talk to about [local government writing].

I would love the opportunity to connect with you for a 20-minute video chat sometime in the next few weeks. I understand you probably keep a busy schedule, so I'm willing to meet before or after business hours, if necessary. Are you available on [day & time slot] or [day & time slot]?

I look forward to hearing back from you.

Best regards,

If John did write an introduction email, below is a template to reply:

[John],
Thank you for the introduction to [Sherry], I really appreciate it.

[Sherry],
Nice to meet you! I'm a student at [UC San Diego] and I'm really interested about starting my career [in the journalism field.] I had a great conversation with [John] last week, and he recommended you as a great person to talk to about [local government writing].

Strategic Relationship Building
Networking with Weak/No Ties

Without a process to follow, connecting with professionals you've never met can be a scary task. Many students are introverts or struggle with imposter syndrome (self-doubt and feeling inadequate) related to connecting with professionals.

Many students think to themselves: *"No professional will want to meet with me"* or *"I might do something wrong that will jeopardize future opportunities, so it's not worth it,"* or *"I'm not a good enough student to be worthy of a professional's time."*

Almost all students—even those more extroverted and those not wrestling with imposter syndrome—struggle with exactly how to optimize their social capital creation efforts.

The great news is that effective outreach with weak/no ties is much less stressful if you follow all the steps and micro-steps of the Career Launch Method. In fact, for many, the process becomes fun and helps build confidence.

Why Professionals Talk to Students

- Empathy toward you and your situation
- Paying forward support they have received in their career
- It's flattering that you'd want to learn from them
- They like to talk about themselves
- It makes them look good to others (spouse, kids, co-workers)
- They may help recruit for positions at their organization

⭐ 10-Day Outreach Strategy

You must follow ALL these micro-steps to maximize your success rate. If you take shortcuts or don't follow this schedule, your chances of getting a "Yes" decrease.

From your Strategic Contact Lists on pages 31-35, **you can choose one person from five different organizations or five people from the same organization.**

(Note: do not count weekends or holidays)

- **Day 1 -** **Initial Email** to contacts 1-5.

- **Day 3 -** **Follow-up Email** to contacts 1-5.

- **Day 5 -** **Call** contacts 1-5.

- **Day 7 -** **LinkedIn message** to contacts 1-5.

- **Day 9 -** **"Give-up" Email** or **Print & Mail a letter.** Include your resume and send in a 9"x12" envelope.

- **Day 10 -** **Stop contacting** the first 5 people and repeat the process with 5 more contacts from your list on pages 31-35.

If you receive a response, great! If you don't receive a response, continue through Day 9 before you stop your outreach.

This is how you separate yourself from other students looking for jobs and internships. You demonstrate that you go above and beyond by being proactive. You are communicating that you are eager for career success and enthusiastic about learning from them.

Professionals will appreciate and respect your professional etiquette and persistence.

Initial Email Template (Day 1) ✉

Sending a clear and concise email is essential to landing a career conversation. The template below has been refined over 10 years based on student data and will optimize your chance of getting a "Yes."

Important: Make sure to customize the email so the professional knows you really care about meeting with them. You can do this by mentioning the name of the college that the person attended or the first company they worked for, in addition to the name of the company they currently work for. **All emails should be sent from your school email address, not your personal email.**

> *Rule of thumb:* for greetings, use first names for professionals in their twenties, and use Mr./Ms. ___ for professionals age 30-40 or older.

Subject Line: [Central College]

Hi [Name*],

I'm a student at [Central College]. I have an assignment this [quarter/semester/summer] to conduct two 20-minute career conversations via video chat or in-person with [companies/organizations] and people that interest me.

You've had a successful career [since you graduated college from _____]. I'd like to learn about your journey from [name of first company after college] to [name of current company] because I'm interested in [_____] as well.

I understand you probably keep a busy schedule, so I'm willing to meet before or after business hours, if necessary. Are you available on [day & time slot] or [day & time slot]?

I look forward to hearing back from you.

Regards,

Sonya Jain
History & Sociology
Central College
phone number
www.linkedin.com/in/_____

Follow-up Email Template (Day 3) ✉

Very few people will respond to the first email, so be prepared to send a follow-up two business days later (weekends don't count). Do not use your previous email. **Start a brand-new email, but use the same subject line.** This follow-up email needs to be concise and polite. Here's the recommended template:

> *Note: More professionals say yes to the follow-up email than the initial email.*

Subject Line: [Central College]

Hi [Name],

I hope your week is going well. I am thrilled at the possibility to meet with you for a 20-minute career conversation for my school assignment.

Can [next Wednesday or Friday] work for you?

Best regards,

Sonya Jain
History & Sociology
Central College
phone number
www.linkedin.com/in/_____

Why pick up the phone?

Many students aren't used to making calls, and this step can be intimidating. However, phone calls are effective precisely because they are becoming less common. **Some professionals will see your emails but only respond to you if you call and leave a voicemail.** Even when a professional works from home, they likely receive work voicemails either on their cell phone or as text in their email.

Make sure you have **set up your voicemail and that your voicemail inbox is not full** before executing this step. Have a friend call your phone number to make sure your voicemail is working correctly in case you get a call back.

Phone Call Template (Day 5) 📞

"Hi _____, this is _____. I'm a student at _____.
   (if they answer, pause and let them acknowledge you)

I have an assignment to conduct two 20-minute career conversations, on a video chat or in-person, with people and organizations that interest me.

You've had a successful career [since you graduated from _____].
I'd like to learn about your journey from [name of first company after college] to [name of company where he/she is working now].

I understand you probably keep a busy schedule, so I'm willing to meet before or after business hours, if necessary. Are you available on _____ or _____?"

(if leaving voicemail) Please call me back at 555-555-5555. That's 555-555-5555. Thank you so much.

Phone Tips

It is unlikely you are going to have a direct line to the employee. You are probably going to be calling a main line and one of two things will likely happen.

1. You'll enter an automated phone tree (eg. "press 1 for...")

2. You will speak with a receptionist. In this scenario, say, "[Maria Smith], please." Notice you aren't reciting the template.

There's a rule in business that goes, "**Don't make a request to someone who can tell you no, but cannot tell you yes.**" Make it sound like you already know the person. Do not say the template above to the receptionist unless you have to.

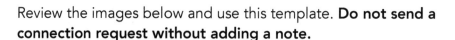

LinkedIn Connection Template (Day 7) 🔗

Review the images below and use this template. **Do not send a connection request without adding a note.**

> Hi [Name],
>
> I'm a student and I have an assignment to conduct two career conversations via video chat or in-person. I'd be thrilled to connect for 20 minutes and learn about your career. I'm willing to connect before or after business hours, if necessary.
>
> Thanks for your consideration,
>
> [your name]

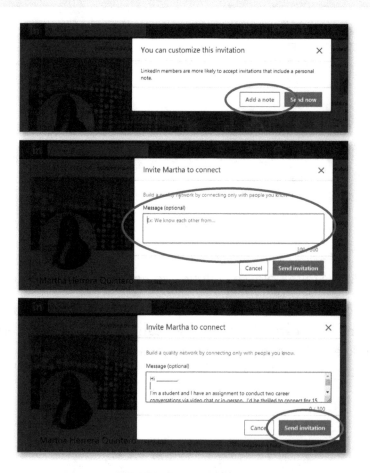

Career Launch Method | 1 | 2 | 3 | **4** | 5 | 6 | 7 | 8

"Give Up" Email (Day 9) 📧

If you know a professional is not working in the office or you can't locate the office address, do this step as an email. Send a follow-up email asking about a potential position, and include your resume as a **PDF attachment.**

Subject Line: Keep me in mind – [Your name], resume attached

Hi [Name],

I know you keep a busy schedule. I hope our paths will cross down the road.

Please keep me in mind for any opportunities and/or forward my attached resume on to a co-worker.

Many thanks,

Sonya Jain
History & Sociology
Central College
phone number
www.linkedin.com/in/_____

"You have to take advantage of

the opportunity of a lifetime in the

lifetime of the opportunity."

\- Eric Thomas

Optional Strategy- Letter In The Mail

If you know the office address of the professional you are contacting, you should **send a letter along with your resume**. This step requires you to print a letter and your resume (ideally on cardstock paper or resume paper), purchase an oversized envelope (9x12) so you don't have to fold your letter or resume, purchase stamps, and then send it in the mail. Below is a template of how to address an envelope to a business.

Address Template

[Company Name]
Attn: [Recipient Name]
[Department/Job Title]
Street Address
City, State Zip Code

What about using Twitter, Instagram, or other social media platforms?

Is it possible to land a career conversation by reaching out in other ways besides the methods above? Yes, it's possible. In certain industries like design, technology, or journalism, these platforms are common and could help you land a career conversation.

We have ten years of data that says the "**10-Day Outreach Strategy**" gives you the optimal chance for success.

The road less traveled produces the best results.

Handling Rebuttals

As you can imagine, most people do not say "Yes" the very first time they reply to you. A lot of the time, people will respond with some kind of objection. They will say something that sounds like a no but isn't actually a "No." These are called rebuttals. Here are the most common rebuttals:

1. "I'm Busy"

Your Response...

> "Connecting with you is more important to me than just completing an assignment. I'm willing to be patient with your schedule. I'd really like to learn about your career and experiences.
>
> Can we find a time next month? If so, when is best for you?
>
> Also, if there is any chance you can meet sooner, I will be flexible with my schedule. Thank you for your consideration."

2. "Can we do this by phone?"

Your Response...

> "Thank you for the follow up. I am excited and grateful for this opportunity.
>
> My professor requires us to complete these career conversations by video chat or in-person. If it is not possible, I am happy to connect by phone.
>
> I understand talking on the phone is better from a time management perspective, however, I hope you will be able to accommodate an in-person visit or video call.
>
> If you can accommodate a meeting [in-person or video call], I can be extremely flexible with the date and time. Thank you for your consideration."

3. "It's not a good time"

Your Response...

"Okay, no problem. I think it would be great to connect with you regardless of my assignment. I'll circle back with you in a month and hopefully it will be a better time for you."

Other Common Questions

- **"Are you looking for a job?"**

Your Response...

"I am looking to learn about your experience, your background, and your company. I want to learn about your career. If you are looking to hire interns/recent grads, I would certainly be interested but that is not the reason for my request."

- **"How did you find my email?"**

Be honest. Tell them exactly where you found the information, i.e. Clearbit, Hunter.io, Rocketreach.co, etc. You can also say you learned about these resources from this workbook.

- **"What questions will you be asking me?"**

Provide a few questions from your list in Step 5, but don't reveal the closing questions from Step 6.

You set up a meeting! Now what?

After a professional agrees to meet with you, **it's your responsibility to send them a calendar invite.** You should assume that the person is busy and that they will need a calendar event to remember your meeting. Use your school email calendar to create a new event and invite the other person's email to that event. The screenshot below shows the "create event" page for Google Calendar.

A standard professional event title is
"[Your name] | [Professional's name] Connect"

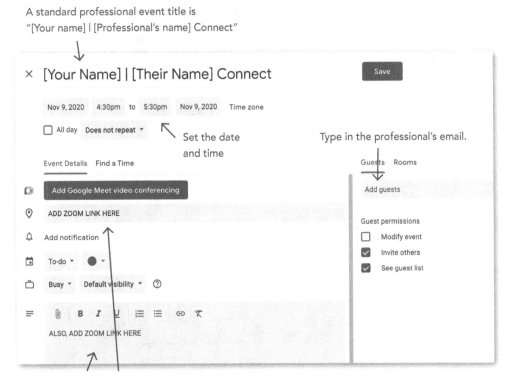

Set the date and time

Type in the professional's email.

If you set up the meeting through Zoom or another provider, paste the link in both the "Location" and "Description" sections.

Make sure to "send" the invitation email.

Take a Deep Breath

Whew! This chapter covered a lot of ground. You now have the templates and strategies you need to begin outreach to professionals. This process takes time, but it is time that could lead to conversations and opportunities that truly change your life.

Students who successfully use career conversations to create relationships with professionals share one thing in common: they consistently set aside time to contact professionals.

Create 30-minute blocks of time in your calendar. This is the time when you will contact professionals. For the first few weeks, I suggest that you set this event to repeat three days per week.

Beginning on the next page, you'll see tracking charts that you can use for the professionals you contact. Write down the information for your first set of five contacts and get started!

▶ What was your biggest takeaway from this outreach section?

_____

_____

_____

▶ How will keep yourself accountable to complete the steps in this chapter and follow the 10-Day Outreach Strategy?

_____

_____

_____

Outreach Tracking for Organization #1: _____

		Additional Contact:	Additional Contact:
Name:			
Job Title:			
Day 1 - Initial Email	☑ Date:	◯ Date:	◯ Date:
Day 3 - Follow-up Email	◯ Date:	◯ Date:	◯ Date:
Day 5 - Phone Call	◯ Date:	◯ Date:	◯ Date:
Day 7 - LinkedIn Message	◯ Date:	◯ Date:	◯ Date:
Day 9 - "Give-up" Email/Letter	◯ Date:	◯ Date:	◯ Date:
Career Conversation Scheduled?	◯ Date:	◯ Date:	◯ Date:

Outreach Tracking for Organization #2: _____

				Additional Contact:	Additional Contact:
Name:					
Job Title:					
Day 1 - Initial Email	Date: ☐	Date: ☐	Date: ☐	Date: ☐	Date: ☐
Day 3 - Follow-up Email	Date: ☐	Date: ☐	Date: ☐	Date: ☐	Date: ☐
Day 5 - Phone Call	Date: ☐	Date: ☐	Date: ☐	Date: ☐	Date: ☐
Day 7 - LinkedIn Message	Date: ☐	Date: ☐	Date: ☐	Date: ☐	Date: ☐
Day 9 - "Give-up" Email/Letter	Date: ☐	Date: ☐	Date: ☐	Date: ☐	Date: ☐
Career Conversation Scheduled?	Date: ☐	Date: ☐	Date: ☐	Date: ☐	Date: ☐

Outreach Tracking for Organization #3: _____

Name:			Additional Contact:	Additional Contact:
Job Title:				
Day 1 - Initial Email	⬜ Date:	⬜ Date:	⬜ Date:	⬜ Date:
Day 3 - Follow-up Email	⬜ Date:	⬜ Date:	⬜ Date:	⬜ Date:
Day 5 - Phone Call	⬜ Date:	⬜ Date:	⬜ Date:	⬜ Date:
Day 7 - LinkedIn Message	⬜ Date:	⬜ Date:	⬜ Date:	⬜ Date:
Day 9 - "Give-up" Email/Letter	⬜ Date:	⬜ Date:	⬜ Date:	⬜ Date:
Career Conversation Scheduled?	⬜ Date:	⬜ Date:	⬜ Date:	⬜ Date:

Outreach Tracking for Organization #4: _____

				Additional Contact:	Additional Contact:
Name:					
Job Title:					
Day 1 - Initial Email	◯ Date:	◯ Date:	◯ Date:	◯ Date:	◯ Date:
Day 3 - Follow-up Email	◯ Date:	◯ Date:	◯ Date:	◯ Date:	◯ Date:
Day 5 - Phone Call	◯ Date:	◯ Date:	◯ Date:	◯ Date:	◯ Date:
Day 7 - LinkedIn Message	◯ Date:	◯ Date:	◯ Date:	◯ Date:	◯ Date:
Day 9 - "Give-up" Email/Letter	◯ Date:	◯ Date:	◯ Date:	◯ Date:	◯ Date:
Career Conversation Scheduled?	◯ Date:	◯ Date:	◯ Date:	◯ Date:	◯ Date:

Outreach Tracking for Organization #5: _____

			Additional Contact:	Additional Contact:
Name:				
Job Title:				
Day 1 - Initial Email	⬭ Date:	⬭ Date:	⬭ Date:	⬭ Date:
Day 3 - Follow-up Email	⬭ Date:	⬭ Date:	⬭ Date:	⬭ Date:
Day 5 - Phone Call	⬭ Date:	⬭ Date:	⬭ Date:	⬭ Date:
Day 7 - LinkedIn Message	⬭ Date:	⬭ Date:	⬭ Date:	⬭ Date:
Day 9 - "Give-up" Email/Letter	⬭ Date:	⬭ Date:	⬭ Date:	⬭ Date:
Career Conversation Scheduled?	⬭ Date:	⬭ Date:	⬭ Date:	⬭ Date:

"Luck is what happens when preparation meets opportunity."

—————

Seneca

"The Career Launch Method has made a huge impact on my life. I use this method for more than just interviews—**if I'm meeting someone new, I keep the key concepts in the back of my mind.** The most impactful tip that I think of often is to plan to arrive generously early. I've had close calls where all of my transportation was running late, but **because I received the tip about arriving extra early, I still arrived on time.**"

Rachel W.
Class of 2023

Step 5

Preparation: Strategies and Best Practices for Career Conversations

The Importance of Preparation

Before conducting a career conversation, you'll want to be prepared with questions and a strategy for making the most of the opportunity and to demonstrate to the professional that you value their time. Career conversations provide a safe environment to learn about a company, role, and career path. Career conversations are also the first step to landing a job or internship that you won't find online or separating yourself from other candidates who, like you, submitted an online application.

While your questions are important, your attire, body language, energy level and timeliness matter just as much. Getting these details right will help you make a good first impression.

What to Wear to Career Conversations

The key is finding clothing that achieves the **3 P's:**
proper fit, polished, and professional

- Collared long-sleeve shirt or professional shirt (including when you're on a video call)
- Jacket (optional depending on industry and weather)

What to Bring (if in-person)

- Portfolio where you can take notes
- 3-4 resumes printed on cardstock
- Laptop or tablet (*if you have one, and if it is applicable for the position you are applying to*)

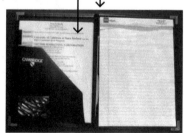

When to Arrive

Video chat → 3-5 minutes early

Phone call → On time

In-person

- Parking Lot → 20-30 mins early
- Office Lobby → 10 mins early

Video Chat Etiquette

In preparation for the career conversation:

- **Prepare small talk questions to start the conversation (see examples below)**
- Dress in professional attire
- Make sure the room is well-lit
- Be mindful of what is visible in your background (if this is a concern, consider a blank wall or virtual background)

During the career conversation:

- Always keep your camera on and make eye contact with the camera when you are speaking
- Be sure to smile and express gratitude 😄
- Don't be too close or too far from the camera
- Don't be monotone; fluctuate your pace and volume to convey enthusiasm

Intentional Small Talk

At the very beginning of your meeting, it's best practice to start with a few easy, non-career questions. This is called making "small talk." The goal of small talk is to establish an authentic connection with the other person before jumping into career-related topics.

- **Start with "How's your day going?"**

  This question is a standard way to begin a conversation. If the person gives a longer 30-second answer, feel free to give an answer that is about that length. If they give a short answer like, "Fine, thanks. How about you?" you should mirror the length of their answer by saying, "Fine, thanks."

- **Ask about a time limit.**

  "I want to make sure I'm respectful of your time. I asked for 20 minutes, do we have a hard stop in 20 minutes?"

  They may say "yes" or "I have 30 minutes blocked out" or simply "no." Knowing your time limit will help you know when to transition to your finishing questions in Step 6.

- **Ask a question that doesn't have to do with their career.**

Touching on a topic besides work allows you to build a more authentic connection. When you are doing research about someone, take note of any hobbies or interests that you find. Avoid asking about polarizing topics like politics and religion, but topics like where they went to college, sports, and local news are fair game. Also, don't dig deep into someone's Facebook or Twitter profiles. However, anything mentioned on an employee biography, LinkedIn profile, or personal website is fair game.

If you are on a video chat or in-person, you can mention anything interesting you see in the person's background like framed pictures, art, posters, etc.

Provide 1 Minute of Background About Yourself

While you should spend most of your time asking the professional questions, sharing a little bit of background information about yourself and why you want to speak with the other person helps them get to know you and be more helpful to you.

Feel free to include any important aspects of your background, interests, experiences, or goals. **The important thing is to keep your background information to about one minute and finish with a question for the professional.**

Tips and Questions to Ask

Keep these tips in mind as you prepare your questions:

Be natural. If a question doesn't feel right, or if you go on a tangent and don't get to ask many of your questions, that's fine. Building a positive relationship is your #1 goal.

Ask relevant follow-up questions. Rather than only sticking to your list of prepared questions, ask follow-up questions when you think of them.

There is no right order to ask the questions on the next page. Ask whichever questions you are most interested in first.

Career Path Question:

- Could you walk me through your career path, starting with your experiences at [name of college they attended] and any internships or jobs you had before your role as [name of current position]?

After someone answers this question, ask a follow-up question about a part of their answer that you found interesting or confusing.

 Job Questions:

- What skills are most important for your job?

- What do you like most about your work? What are you excited about right now?

- What is challenging about your work?

Company/Organization Questions:

- What is the culture like at this company?

- What kinds of opportunities for connection, mentorship and growth does your organization provide?

- What does your company do to provide resources and opportunities to employees from diverse backgrounds?

Industry Questions:

- What advice would you give someone starting out on this career path?

- What is the best way to find a job/internship in this industry?

- What didn't you know before you got into this industry, company, or job function that you wish someone had told you?

Transition Statement and Question:

- It's a good idea to say, "Let me know if I can be a resource for you or your organization in any way in the future."

- Would you mind if I stay in touch periodically?

What to do if the professional is late or doesn't show up to your meeting

Try not to act disappointed, frustrated, or angry, and maintain your enthusiasm. You never know what someone else is working on, and you should be grateful they are taking the time to meet with you. The good news is that if the person is late or does not show up, they will likely be even more responsive in the future and appreciate your graciousness.

For a video chat or phone call, wait 5 minutes past the scheduled start time for your meeting. If the professional hasn't communicated with you about why they are late, you should send them a short email similar to the template below.

Subject Line: Need to reschedule?

Hi [Name],

Do you need a few more minutes to join our meeting, or would you prefer to reschedule later this week or next week?

Thanks,

[your name]

"It takes as much energy to

wish as it does to plan."

- Eleanor Roosevelt

Preparation Questions

▶ Consider the activities and conversations you have scheduled in the near future. Think about the people involved and how you want those people to feel after you interact with them. Think about what kind of energy, emotions, and state of being you'll need to embody to create your intended outcomes.

Write down anything that comes to mind below.

_____

_____

_____

_____

▶ During your research, what did you learn about the professionals as human beings (i.e. hobbies, interests, favorite teams, where they went to college, etc.)?

_____

_____

_____

_____

▶ Which questions do you want to prioritize?

_____

_____

_____

_____

"While one person hesitates because they feel inferior, the other is busy making mistakes and becoming superior."

Henry C. Link

"The Career Launch Method was absolutely pivotal in my career. It taught me how to use cold calling and cold emailing techniques to secure career conversations and build relationships at companies where I had no connections prior. **I completed 18 career conversations and secured four job offers before graduation.**"

Jess R.
Class of 2023

Step 6

Advanced Preparation: Turn Career Conversations into Interviews, Referrals, Recommendations and Mentorship

Know Your Goal(s)

Before conducting a career conversation, consider what you hope to get out of the conversation. You should start every conversation with small talk, then ask questions you genuinely wonder about the person's career path and professional life. At the end of the conversation, **tailor your questions to your goal(s).**

Remember: **you must clearly ask for what you want!** Many professionals will wait for you to ask for a certain type of help, not because they are testing you or withholding anything, but because they aren't sure of your goals beyond having the career conversation.

Primary Goal: Explore career options

Every career conversation will help you explore career options and build your network, regardless of any other goals. At the end of your conversation, **you should ask the professional to connect you with anyone else they know who could be helpful to you.**

It's best if you are **specific** in your request. For example, perhaps you have a conversation with a school teacher, and you're also interested in becoming a principal down the road. Rather than asking if the person knows "anyone who could help you," you could ask if they would be willing to introduce you to the principal at their school for a conversation.

There is little downside (and nearly unlimited upside) to asking for connections to other people. You can say:

- If I want to learn more about [this job type, industry, organization, topic, etc.], who are two people in your network that I should connect with for a career conversation like this?

In addition to exploring career options and building your network, you may have one or more of the following goals.

Optional Goal: Land a formal interview

Ask this four-question sequence near the end of the conversation if you are interested in a formal **job or internship opportunity**:

1. What qualities or characteristics do you and the organization look for in an ideal [intern/recent grad] candidate?

2. Can I take a minute to tell you a little more about myself?

   If they say yes, keep your response to 2 minutes or less so they stay engaged. Use the applicable parts of what they just said about an ideal candidate in your description about yourself.

3. Based on what you've learned about me, do you think I'm someone that would be a good fit at this organization?

4. Who do you recommend I speak with? What do you suggest as next steps?

> **Note:** Be sure to review the internship/job opportunities on the organization's website (if any) prior to your career conversation so you can reference any positions you're specifically interested in.

Optional Goal: Get a recommendation

A study of over 60,000 applications found that candidates who get a referral from a current employee are **12 times more likely** to be hired than applicants who only apply online.

Almost all organizations have some method for employee referrals. Unless you feel like the professional you're meeting with is disinterested or that the conversation is not going well, you should ask one or both of these questions at the end of the conversation:

- I know we just met, but based on the little bit you know about me, would you be willing to recommend me as a candidate for an internship (or job)?

- If I receive a formal interview, would you be willing to put in a good word for me?

Optional Goal: Develop a mentoring relationship

You don't need to ask someone to "be your mentor" to establish a mentoring relationship. Professionals will be more likely to mentor you if you come to them with specific and relevant questions when you face an important decision, transition, or opportunity.

It's totally fine and normal to have a variety of mentors that you mostly speak to when you need support on something specific. If you develop a mentoring relationship where you connect with a certain frequency, that's great too. The important thing is to **use the follow-up methods in Step 7 to establish a longer-term relationship.**

"How would you prepare if you knew that tomorrow you would meet someone that would change your life?"

- Dan Casetta

▶ Which goal(s) are most relevant to you right now?

_____

_____

_____

_____

_____

Expect the Unexpected

You should be prepared for a wide variety of outcomes during your career conversation. Although some of these scenarios are uncommon, it's always best to be prepared.

Not all career conversations will be life-changing. But I can tell you from my experience with students that it happens more often than you might imagine. In general, professionals like to help students who reach out, so they likely already have a positive impression of you before your meeting.

Here are some scenarios to be prepared for, all of which usually work to your benefit if you are prepared and adaptable:

- **The conversation goes longer than planned**

  Some people will have a hard stop at the 20 minutes you asked for, and others won't. Often, if the person has time and the conversation is going well, it can go significantly longer than your allotted time, which is great. Just make sure you have room in your schedule for the conversation to go long, and be respectful of the person's time.

- **Interview on the spot**

  During some career conversations, professionals might ask you questions about your interests or experiences. You should always be ready to answer these interview-style questions. Interview best practices will be reviewed in Step 8.

- **Other people join or you get an office tour** *(if in-person)*

  One of my former students, Marcus, had a career conversation with the former CFO of Netflix and at the end, the CFO said, "Aren't you going to ask me for a tour?" If you are meeting in-person, ask for a tour. You'll get a feel for the company culture and you might be introduced to other professionals along the way with whom you could schedule career conversations.

"People will forget what you said. People will forget what you did. But people will never forget how you made them feel."

Maya Angelou

"The Career Launch Method taught me that failure is a critical component of eventual success. I contacted many people and only landed three conversations. And yet, **I consider that semester to have been extremely successful. Who cares how many times you get no response or rejected?** My bold approach helped me land a marketing and operations internship at a fast-growing startup after my freshman year."

 Stefan S.
Class of 2021

Effective Follow-Up: Differentiate Yourself and Build Long-Term Relationships

Effectively Follow Up After Your Career Conversations

Some students forget to send a thank-you email, which is unacceptable. And some students believe that if they send a follow-up email within a few days they have "effectively followed up."

Not at Career Launch. Effective follow-up is a multi-step process.

 ## 1. Next Day ✉

Send your **thank-you email between 6-7 a.m. the next day** (even if your career conversation is on a Friday).

Subject Line: Thank you from [First Name Last Name]

Dear [_____],

It was great to talk with you yesterday. I really appreciate you making time for me.

I learned so much. In particular, I enjoyed what you said about [_____]. I need to give that more thought as I transition from college into a career.

It was also great to learn about [_____]. I appreciate your advice. I'll certainly be mindful of that going forward. [or, "I'll start working on that right away."]

[(*if applicable*) Thank you for encouraging me to stay in touch and offering to introduce me to _____].

I have attached my resume below and would appreciate you keeping me in mind for any positions that might be a good fit.

Again, many thanks.

- [First name]

[Email Signature]

2. Two-Three Business Days Later ✉

If you have the office address of the person you spoke with, craft a **handwritten thank-you note**, put it in an envelope with a stamp, and mail it to their office.

Dear [_____],

Thanks again for your time [earlier this week].

I've already [started thinking about this, or started doing that] and I'm excited [_____].

Learning about [be specific, not general, about one of the main things you learned] was really valuable. I'll certainly keep that in mind as I enter the workforce.

With gratitude,

[First name Last name]

Example of an addressed thank-you note to an organization:

[Organization Name]
Attn: [Recipient Name]
[Department or Job Title]
Street Address
City, State Zip Code

If you do not have the address of the adult/professional, you can send an **online thank-you card** instead of a handwritten card. **Try searching "Free Thank You E-cards."**

3) Touch points 1 month, 3 months, 6 months later

This is when you need to keep the relationship alive. Here are some great ways to stay in touch with past connections:

The "Thought of You" Method

This type of message is sent to tell someone that you were reminded of them based on something from your conversation. For example, maybe you have a professor who speaks about the professional's industry or job function during class. Or maybe you discussed a common love of science fiction books during your career conversation. You can send them a short message saying that you thought of them.

Template #1:

Hi _____,

Thanks again for taking the time to tell me about your career path [earlier this year].

[In class/At my job/At my internship recently], we had a conversation about [water purification methods] and it reminded me of the [project] you'd mentioned you were working on. It's exciting work you're doing!

I hope you're doing well,
[your name]

Template #2:

Hi _____,

Thanks again for taking the time to tell me about your career path [earlier this year].

I recently [finished reading a book/read an article/watched a webinar, completed a certification], and it reminded me of our conversation about [topic].

I hope all is well,
[your name]

The Reflection Method

Another easy way to keep in touch with professionals is by sending messages around key milestones in the calendar; for example, the end of the semester/academic year and holidays such as Thanksgiving and New Year's.

In these messages, you can say that you have been reflecting on your conversation and continue to be grateful that they made themselves available to talk with you.

Template #1:

> Hi _____,
>
> As I finish my [program/first year/sophomore year/junior year/senior year/etc.], I was reflecting on what I learned from our conversation and wanted to thank you again for taking the time to tell me about your career.
>
> I hope you're doing well!
>
> Best,
> [your name]

Template #2:

> Hi _____,
>
> As we approach [the start of the new year/Thanksgiving], I was reflecting on what I learned from our conversation and wanted to thank you again for taking the time [to give me advice on my career (or job search, etc.)].
>
> I hope you're doing well!
>
> Best,
> [your name]

Invite the Professional to be a Guest Speaker

If you participate in an on-campus student organization (or are taking a relevant class), you can invite the professional to be a guest speaker or lead a workshop related to their field of expertise or career path.

Hi _____, I hope you're doing well!

I'm the [Vice President/Treasurer/a member] of [club name] and we are hosting [event description].

Would you be interested in [participating in the panel/giving a brief presentation] to the club on [date]?

Thanks for your consideration,
[John]

[Email Signature]

The Social Media Method

This method relies on social media to form brief interactions that keep you at the top of a professional's mind.

If the professional posts on LinkedIn, you can comment on their post. If they have commented on someone else's post, you can reply to their comment.

Many professionals maintain an active presence on LinkedIn even if they don't regularly post or comment. In this case, you can share a relevant post or article with them through a private message. Share the link and a few sentences about why you thought this would be of interest to them, based on your overlapping interests. Remember, do not end with a question.

Career Conversation Notes

Name:	Organization:
Job Title:	Date:

Goals:

Most Important Takeaways:

_____

_____

_____

_____

_____

_____

Other people to talk to:

_____

_____

Next Steps:		Done?
_____		☐
_____		☐

Thank-you email next morning:	☐	Handwritten thank-you note 3 days later:	☐
Add on LinkedIn 10-14 days later:	☐	1, 3 & 6 month follow-ups:	☐ ☐ ☐

Career Conversation Notes

Name:	Organization:
Job Title:	Date:

Goals:

Most Important Takeaways:

_____

_____

_____

_____

_____

_____

_____

Other people to talk to:

_____

_____

Next Steps:	Done?
_____	☐
_____	☐

Thank-you email next morning: ☐	Handwritten thank-you note 3 days later: ☐
Add on LinkedIn 10-14 days later: ☐	1, 3 & 6 month follow-ups: ☐ ☐ ☐

Career Conversation Notes

Name:	Organization:
Job Title:	Date:

Goals:

Most Important Takeaways:

_____

_____

_____

_____

_____

_____

_____

Other people to talk to:

_____

_____

Next Steps: Done?

_____ ☐

_____ ☐

Thank-you email next morning: ☐	Handwritten thank-you note 3 days later: ☐
Add on LinkedIn 10-14 days later: ☐	1, 3 & 6 month follow-ups: ☐ ☐ ☐

Career Conversation Notes

Name:	Organization:
Job Title:	Date:

Goals:

Most Important Takeaways:

_____

_____

_____

_____

_____

_____

_____

Other people to talk to:

_____

_____

Next Steps: Done?

_____   ▢

_____   ▢

Thank-you email next morning: ▢	Handwritten thank-you note 3 days later: ▢
Add on LinkedIn 10-14 days later: ▢	1, 3 & 6 month follow-ups: ▢ ▢ ▢

Career Conversation Notes

Name:	Organization:
Job Title:	Date:

Goals:

Most Important Takeaways:

Other people to talk to:

Next Steps: Done?

Thank-you email next morning: ☐	Handwritten thank-you note 3 days later: ☐
Add on LinkedIn 10-14 days later: ☐	1, 3 & 6 month follow-ups: ☐ ☐ ☐

Career Conversation Notes

Name:	Organization:
Job Title:	Date:

Goals:

Most Important Takeaways:

_____

_____

_____

_____

_____

_____

Other people to talk to:

_____

_____

Next Steps:	Done?
_____	☐
_____	☐

Thank-you email next morning: ☐	Handwritten thank-you note 3 days later: ☐
Add on LinkedIn 10-14 days later: ☐	1, 3 & 6 month follow-ups: ☐ ☐ ☐

Career Conversation Notes

Name:	Organization:
Job Title:	Date:

Goals:

Most Important Takeaways:

_____

_____

_____

_____

_____

_____

Other people to talk to:

_____

_____

Next Steps: Done?

_____ ☐

_____ ☐

| Thank-you email next morning: ☐ | Handwritten thank-you note 3 days later: ☐ |
| Add on LinkedIn 10-14 days later: ☐ | 1, 3 & 6 month follow-ups: ☐ ☐ ☐ |

Career Conversation Notes

Name:	Organization:
Job Title:	Date:

Goals:

Most Important Takeaways:

_____

_____

_____

_____

_____

_____

Other people to talk to:

_____

_____

Next Steps: Done?

_____ ☐

_____ ☐

Thank-you email next morning: ☐	Handwritten thank-you note 3 days later: ☐
Add on LinkedIn 10-14 days later: ☐	1, 3 & 6 month follow-ups: ☐ ☐ ☐

Career Conversation Notes

Name:	Organization:
Job Title:	Date:

Goals:

Most Important Takeaways:

_____

_____

_____

_____

_____

_____

_____

Other people to talk to:

_____

_____

Next Steps:	Done?
_____	☐
_____	☐

Thank-you email next morning:	☐	Handwritten thank-you note 3 days later:	☐
Add on LinkedIn 10-14 days later:	☐	1, 3 & 6 month follow-ups:	☐ ☐ ☐

"It's not what you know that makes the difference. It's what you do with what you know that makes the difference."

Dr. Julie White

"Having seen the Career Launch Method be so successful at building relationships with professionals, I had a lot of faith in Sean's advice on interviews as well. I incorporated stories into my answers and I felt great about my interviews. **A few weeks later, I got a call letting me know I got the internship!** I have so much gratitude for learning the Career Launch Method which led to an early win during college."

Yevin L.
Class of 2023

Step 8

Ace the Job Interview: Convey Your Value and Land the Position

Congrats, you landed an interview! How should you prepare? This section gives you some tips to get started. Visit your school's career center webpage for more resources and/or consult with one of your school's career counselors.

Types of Interviews

- Behavioral   *(questions about you and your experiences)*
- Case-based   *(questions about a scenario or situation)*
- Group work   *(a task where you must collaborate with others)*
- Assignment-based   *(a take-home or in-person task you complete)*
- Test for hard skills   *(common for technical roles)*

Applying the STAR Method

The STAR Method is a tool for answering behavioral interview questions.

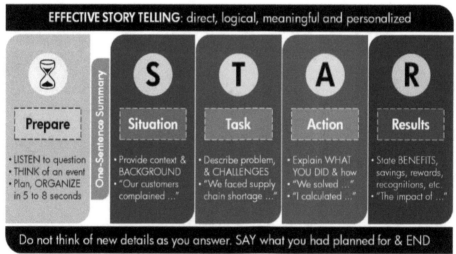

EFFECTIVE STORY TELLING: direct, logical, meaningful and personalized

One-Sentence Summary

Prepare
- LISTEN to question
- THINK of an event
- Plan, ORGANIZE in 5 to 8 seconds

S **Situation**
- Provide context & BACKGROUND
- "Our customers complained ..."

T **Task**
- Describe problem, & CHALLENGES
- "We faced supply chain shortage ..."

A **Action**
- Explain WHAT YOU DID & how
- "We solved ..."
- "I calculated ..."

R **Results**
- State BENEFITS, savings, rewards, recognitions, etc.
- "The impact of ..."

Do not think of new details as you answer. SAY what you had planned for & END

http://www.RightAttitudes.com

"The best preparation for tomorrow is doing your best today."

- H. Jackson Brown, Jr.

Common Interview Formats

- **Automated**

A computer system asks you to turn on your camera and microphone and then record your answers to automated questions.

- **Phone**

Common for first-round interviews. Make sure to listen well, take your time and show enthusiasm through your voice.

- **Video Call**

Test your video and audio in a quiet space before beginning. Keep other tabs on your computer closed and smile and nod to show you are listening.

- **In-person**

The "what to bring" and "when to arrive" sections from Step 5 apply here.

Interview Best Practices

- **Practice your answers out loud**

Thinking about your answers or writing them down is not enough. You should practice saying your answers out loud, either to the mirror, a friend, or a virtual mock interview system (your career center may have access to a tool like this). Practice makes perfect!

- **Make eye contact most of the time**

You should not be looking down or off into the distance when answering a question. Look at the other person, or if you are on a video call, look directly into the camera.

- **Don't rely on your notes**

It's okay to glance at notes you have prepared or write a few notes during your interview, but you should not be looking at your notes for more than a second here or there. Your interviewer wants to hear from you, not your notes.

Two Questions You Must Answer (even if they aren't asked)

1. Why do you want the position?

This is somewhat of a trick question. **Too often students answer this question selfishly about how the job will benefit them.**

They might say, "your company has a great training program," or "this job will be a great stepping stone to achieving my long-term career goals" or "your office is close to where I live" or "I like that I can work remotely." Although these answers are acceptable as secondary reasons, they overemphasize what you want.

What you should do is **state why you want the role in context of how you will benefit the organization.**

Say something like, "I'm confident that I can excel at this job because I will be able to apply my creativity and adaptability to contribute to the design team. In my last role, I did ____ which contributed _____." Then say something like, "I also know your company has a great training program which will help me grow and succeed in the role."

2. Why are you the best person for the position?

This question is not often asked directly, but you should be discussing your skills and why you would excel in the role in almost every answer you give.

The organization is likely interviewing dozens of candidates for the position. How are you going to contribute? The stories you share in your answers should highlight how your role in a previous situation contributed to a positive outcome. Perhaps you don't have many accomplishments to point toward. In that case, speak about examples of your best attributes, characteristics, and virtues.

Common Interview Questions

For each of these questions, write down a few words or bullet points that will remind you which story and key points you want to emphasize. There's no need to script your answers, but you should be prepared for any of these questions.

- **Tell me about yourself.**

Note: this is often the first question asked and is incredibly open-ended. You should prepare an answer that highlights your key skills and accomplishments. Practice this answer out loud and aim for 2-3 minutes.

- **Why this job/company/role?**

Your answer shouldn't focus on why the job is good for you, but on why you know you'll be a good fit for the position. You can also talk about how your personal values and motivation align with the company's values or mission.

▶ How will you answer "Tell me about yourself?"

_____

_____

_____

_____

▶ How will you answer "Why this job?" (this answer will likely change for different roles you interview for)

_____

_____

_____

_____

More Interview Questions to Prepare For

Personal Questions:

- What are your strengths?
- What are your weaknesses?
- How would your classmates/professors describe you?
- Where do you see yourself in 5 years?
- What is an accomplishment that you are proud of?
- What motivates you? What are you passionate about?
- Do you prefer working alone or in teams?
- What type of work environment do you prefer?
- How do you deal with pressure or stressful situations?

"Tell me about a time when..." Questions:

- ... you disagreed with your manager.
- ... you demonstrated leadership skills.
- ... you influenced an important decision.
- ... you faced a conflict in a team.
- ... you had to make a decision under pressure.
- ... something unexpected happened and you had to adapt.
- ... you failed. What did you learn?

The Importance of Stories

The best way to ace any behavioral interview is to choose and **write down 6-8 stories** that you can use to answer a wide range of questions. Your stories should include gratitude, authenticity, enthusiasm and/or accountability. When telling your stories, be sure to mention the situation, actions you took that demonstrated your skills, and results you achieved.

Preparing your stories ahead of time ensures that you are concise, only sharing the most relevant information. You shouldn't take more than 2-3 minutes to answer a question, so you need to practice telling your stories with the most important details.

Here are a few topics to brainstorm stories around:

- A time you showed leadership without being in a leadership position
- A time when you persuaded someone to act
- A time you failed and what you learned
- A time you had to quickly adapt or learn something new
- A professional or academic accomplishment you are proud of
- How you solved a difficult problem
- A time you worked in a team to accomplish a goal

After you write down your stories, **practice telling them out loud.**

On the next two pages, you'll find examples of how to take notes on your stories. The pages after the examples give you space to write down your stories and what skills they demonstrate.

Prepare to ask your own questions!

During, or at the end of, most behavioral interviews, you will get a chance to ask your own questions about the organization, position, your interviewer, or the work you might do. There are no right or wrong questions to ask, but you should be genuinely curious and do your research ahead of time to ask smart and thoughtful questions.

The quality of your questions says a lot about you as an applicant.

Effective Job Interview Follow-up

It's crucial that you send a thank-you email after your interview. Reference the methods in Step 7.

If you meet with multiple people, it's typically best practice to send individual emails to each person.

Examples of Interview Stories
(in note form)

1. **Small business marketing project**
   - I took control of our disorganized team and politely delegated tasks and responsibilities based on the strengths of the team. I developed a plan and schedule for the quarter-long project and got continual advice from the professor. I played a key role to earn our team an A, and there was minimal friction while helping drive traffic to the small business restaurant.
   - *Skills Shown:* leadership, teamwork

2. **Supporting family after brother's injury**
   - Last year, my younger brother broke his collarbone, difficult for our family because of the medical bills and frequent trips to the doctor's office. I would help get him to rehab appointments, make dinner when my single mom was still out working, and organize medical forms that mom needed to sign. Brother eventually healed and I think it brought us closer as a family and helped me take responsibility and appreciate medial workers.
   - *Skills Shown:* loyalty, humility, resilience, responsibility

3. **2-month contract at Zume**
   - After spending 6 months learning how to program I had a pact with the CEO to start on a contract to see if I could make it. I was given complex problems that were overwhelming. With no training or support I continued to teach myself how to perform tasks at hand (API scripts) working day and night and eventually was awarded a position.
   - *Skills Shown:* perseverance, humility, eager to learn, work ethic, resilience

4. Teaching myself to code for analyst position

- Created a life action plan, researching people with jobs I could see myself in that aligned with interests. Spent all my free time for 6 months between/after class learning skills for data analysis. I watched YouTube, read books, took online courses and sacrificed social life and "senior year fun" for the betterment of my career and personal growth.

- *Skills Shown:* self-improvement, eager to learn, work ethic, resilience

5. Tutoring elementary students in math

- I taught weekly math lessons to a third-grader and a fifth-grader in my town. In addition to helping them with their homework, I helped teach them concepts they were weaker on and provided additional study materials when they were ahead of where they needed to be. Sometimes motivating them was a challenge, good experience balancing being liked and respected.

- *Skills Shown:* collaboration, leadership, empathy

Reminder: this workbook is a complement to Career Launch's micro-learning programs and to the *Launch Your Career* book.

For a deeper dive into any of the eight steps, reference the micro-learning and/or the book.

Write Down Your Stories in Note Form

▶ Story 1:

_____

_____

_____

_____

_____

Skills shown:

_____

_____

▶ Story 2:

_____

_____

_____

_____

_____

Skills shown:

_____

_____

Choose stories that show your leadership, problem-solving, growth, collaboration, perseverance, or how you overcame failure or challenges.

▶ Story 3:

_____

_____

_____

_____

_____

_____

Skills shown: _____

_____

▶ Story 4:

_____

_____

_____

_____

_____

_____

Skills shown: _____

_____

Components of a Job Offer

Many students focus solely on salary and the job position when considering a job offer. We recommend you consider all of the following before accepting an offer:

1. Salary

The amount of money the organization will be paying you. This can be an hourly rate or a yearly amount.

2. Standard Benefits

Consider benefits like health insurance, dental, vision, and retirement plans (401k, etc.).

3. Vacation Time or Paid Time Off (PTO)

PTO can include all vacation, personal, sick, and holiday time.

4. Work-Life Balance 💻

Work may be in-person, remote, or hybrid. Learn about the hours you are expected to work each week.

5. Additional Perks 🐷

Other benefits can include child care, a signing bonus, stock options, pensions, life insurance, use of a company car, additional work from home days/flexible work schedule, etc.

Salary & Compensation Negotiation

Negotiating your pay and overall compensation can make a huge difference over the course of your career, and it's well worth having an uncomfortable---for most people---conversation.

Even if you don't get what you ask for, negotiating---using the etiquette on the following pages---is worth it because you demonstrate that you are someone who **understands how to appropriately engage in difficult conversations, which is a sign of a future leader.**

While it's impossible to plan for every potential scenario, here are a couple best practices along with several recommendations on how to answer questions with professional etiquette.

Two Golden Rules

Entry-Level Compensation Negotiation

1. Don't be the first person to give a number or a range

> **The logic behind rule #1:**
>
> If you give a number that's **below** what the organization was expecting, they will likely think you'll be happy with this amount, and thus, you may be offered less than you would have been otherwise (even though there are laws that are supposed to prevent this).
>
> If you give a number or range that is too **high**, they might eliminate you from the interview process because they know they won't be able to afford you and it doesn't make sense for you to meet with other people in the interview process. Therefore, it is best practice to politely answer these questions without giving a number or range.

If any recruiters or hiring managers ask about your salary requirements before you receive a job offer, you should avoid saying a number or range. Let's take a look at this example:

> Recruiter: *"What are your salary requirements?"*
>
> You: *"At this point in the process, I'm focused on finding the right fit. I'm confident that when I do, salary and compensation will not be an issue."*
>
> Recruiter: *"Thanks for sharing. My boss/software program requires us to have a salary or range from our candidates. What is yours?"*
>
> You: *"What is your range for this position?"*

If they give a number or range, you simply respond by saying:

> You: *"Thanks for sharing. That won't be an issue."*

If they don't answer the question directly, they will likely say, "The range is based on qualifications and experience." To which you should reply:

> You: *"I understand. Of everyone that has been hired for this position in the past two years, what is the lowest and highest salary and compensation someone has received?"*

117

2. Avoid negotiating before you have a written offer

> ### 👤 The logic behind rule #2:
>
> As a job candidate, you likely do not have much leverage. In many cases, there are lots of candidates applying for the job and only limited jobs available. The employer has the leverage UNTIL they provide you an offer in writing (not just a verbal offer).
>
> Many employers will strategically provide a verbal offer to ask you to commit verbally on the spot because it is more difficult for you to ask for higher salary or benefits if you say "Yes."

This is another reason you want to follow Rule #1 and avoid giving a number or a range.

If you have a call or meeting where you receive a verbal offer, you should **avoid committing on the spot even if you are sure you'll accept the job.** It is best practice to ask for the offer in writing.

Avoid negotiating over email

Receiving a Verbal Offer

You want to say something like:

> You: *"Thank you for this offer. I'm really excited about joining the team. My [professors/family members/mentors] have told me it's best practice to review an offer letter in writing and sleep on it before signing.*
>
> *I imagine that you will be sending an offer in writing soon, is that correct?"*

In this way, you express your enthusiasm about the position while giving yourself time to review the offer.

Conversation after Receiving the Written Offer

After you have had a chance to review the written offer, you will want to set up a video chat or in-person meeting to inquire about your compensation package.

In the meeting, start by expressing gratitude for the offer and asking genuine questions about your job role, organization, or work environment. Then ask the following questions:

> You: *"Do you have any flexibility in regards to salary/compensation?"*
>
> Recruiter: *"Possibly. What do you have in mind?"*
>
> You: *"Based on my research of comparable positions on [name the credible website where you found the information] and the value I believe I will add to the team, I think [a salary of $_____ would be appropriate] or [a bonus of $_____ would be appropriate] or [$_____ for moving expense would be more suitable], etc.*
>
> *Can that work for you?*

Regardless of the answer you receive to your question about compensation flexibility, there's another question you should ask:

> You: *"Assuming I do an outstanding job in this role, what is the opportunity for my compensation to increase at the end of my first year and second year?*

The other person's answer to this question will allow you to know what to expect for your near-term earning potential. This will give you peace of mind and insight into your short-term earnings opportunity. Asking this question after you start your job can be awkward. However, this is the optimal time to ask.

"Knowledge is not power. Knowledge is potential power. Action is power."

Tony Robbins

"The Career Launch Method taught me that **resilience and relationships are two of the most important things** to have in any stage of your career. I am an introverted person, but with step-by-step guidance, I became more comfortable with the idea of introducing myself to people I didn't know. With the method and resilience, I have been able to earn multiple jobs and internships.

Sarina J.
Class of 2016

Resume & Cover Letter Best Practices

Crafting an Effective Resume

Your resume provides a snapshot of your experiences and accomplishments to employers. Employers will skim your resume in 6-30 seconds, so format the document in a way that is easy to digest.

This section gives you some tips to get started. **Visit your school's career center webpage for more resources.**

Resume Basics:

- One page
- Always send as a PDF
- No mistakes (ask friends/family to proofread)
- Must-have sections: Education, Experience, Skills/Interests

Resume Writing Principles:

- Use strong verbs and specific language
- Quantify your accomplishments, i.e. add numbers whenever possible
- Include your most impressive accomplishments
- Show how your work led to a final impact

Each work experience entry should have 2-3 bullet points. **Make sure to show the reader why your actions mattered, ideally within the first 5 words of the bullet.** It's better to have a long bullet point that shows your impressive impact than a short bullet that lacks relevance.

Weak bullet point: "Analyzed customer data and created data visualizations for the management team."

Strong bullet point using numbers and showing impact: "Identified $200k in new sales opportunities for executives based on customer data" or "Helped improve customer satisfaction by 40% by creating 3 strategies with visualizations to reduce transaction time."

Resume Design and Purposes

You may want to create two different versions of your resume.

If you are submitting a resume online, ensure it's created using Google Docs or Microsoft Word, and then submit it as a PDF, so that automated resume software will be able to recognize the formatting.

If you will be sending your resume via email or handing it out in-person, consider creating a second version that is designed to **capture a professional's attention and emphasizes your best attributes.**

Below is an example of this two-version approach. Your school's career center likely has more resume samples or resources.

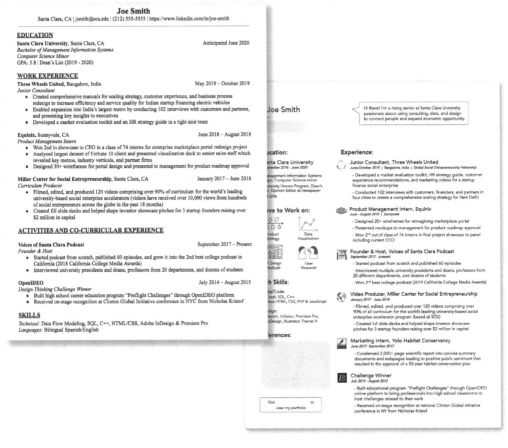

Resume Example #1 - ATS Compatible

Many organizations use **Applicant Tracking Systems (ATS)** to manage the application process. This is a system that collects, scans, and ranks your resume to make the hiring process easier for recruiters.

The resume below uses simple formatting with clear headings.

Joe Smith

Santa Clara, CA | jsmith@scu.edu | (212) 555-5555 | https://www.linkedin.com/in/joe-smith

---

EDUCATION

Santa Clara University, Santa Clara, CA   Anticipated June 2020
Bachelor of Management Information Systems
Computer Science Minor
GPA: 3.8 | Dean's List (2019 - 2020)

WORK EXPERIENCE

Three Wheels United, Bangalore, India   May 2019 – October 2019
Junior Consultant
- Created comprehensive manuals for scaling strategy, customer experience, and business process redesign to increase efficiency and service quality for Indian startup financing electric vehicles
- Enabled expansion into India's largest metro by conducting 102 interviews with customers and partners, and presenting key insights to executives
- Developed a market evaluation toolkit and an HR strategy guide in a tight-knit team

Equinix, Sunnyvale, CA   June 2018 – August 2018
Product Management Intern
- Won 2nd in showcase to CEO in a class of 74 interns for enterprise marketplace portal redesign project
- Analyzed largest dataset of Fortune 10 client and presented visualization deck to senior sales staff which revealed key metros, industry verticals, and partner firms
- Designed 30+ wireframes for portal design and presented to management for product roadmap approval

Miller Center for Social Entrepreneurship, Santa Clara, CA   January 2017 – June 2018
Curriculum Producer
- Filmed, edited, and produced 120 videos comprising over 90% of curriculum for the world's leading university-based social enterprise accelerators (videos have received over 10,000 views from hundreds of social entrepreneurs across the globe in the past 18 months)
- Created fill slide decks and helped shape investor showcase pitches for 3 startup founders raising over $2 million in capital

ACTIVITIES AND CO-CURRICULAR EXPERIENCE

Voices of Santa Clara Podcast   September 2017 – Present
Founder & Host
- Started podcast from scratch, published 60 episodes, and grew it into the 2nd best college podcast in California (2018 California College Media Awards)
- Interviewed university presidents and deans, professors from 20 departments, and dozens of students

OpenIDEO   July 2014 – August 2015
Design Thinking Challenge Winner
- Built high school career education program "Preflight Challenges" through OpenIDEO platform
- Received on-stage recognition at Clinton Global Initiative conference in NYC from Nicholas Kristof

SKILLS

Technical: Data Flow Modeling, SQL, C++, HTML/CSS, Adobe InDesign & Premiere Pro
Languages: Bilingual Spanish/English

Resume Example #2

The resume below is more creative and can be added to your online portfolio, LinkedIn profile, as an additional document to an online application, or used when printing.

However, this resume is not ATS-friendly.

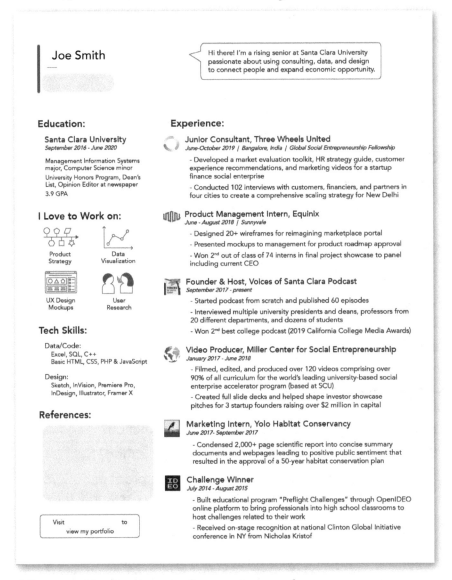

**These are just two out of many types of resumes.
Consult your career center for more resources.**

Cover Letters

Cover Letters are less common and less important than resumes, but a great cover letter could be the detail that separates you from the competition. The purpose of the cover letter is to discuss the skills that make you a good fit and showcase why you believe you are confident you will excel in the role.

Tip: Use the job description of the role you are applying for as a guide.

Cover Letter Do's

- One page, sufficient spacing
- Use "I" not "we" language
- Customize for each company and position
- Heavily proofread
- Relate your experience to the job requirements

Cover Letter Don'ts

- Repeat the exact content from your resume
- Write in a casual tone
- Focus exclusively on yourself instead of how you can add value to the company

Tip: Utilize Sub-headers

- **Body paragraph 1:** Answer "why this job function?"
- **Body paragraph 2**: Answer "why this organization?"

  In the body paragraphs, provide narrative proof of how you have added value in the past and how you can apply these skills in a role with the organization. As with your resume, this section should show the results and impact you can create.

  Your cover letter should show how your skills and interests align with the values of the organization and make you a great fit for the position you are applying for.

Cover Letter Sample

Joe Smith

Santa Clara, CA 95050 | (212) 555-5555 | jsmith@scu.edu

15 February 2018

LinkedIn
222 2nd Street
San Francisco, CA 94105

Dear Hiring Committee,

I am excited to be applying for a Sales Development Specialist position with LinkedIn.

Why Sales?

Last summer, I had the opportunity to work as a Sales Development Representative for a high-growth tech company. After just a few weeks in the position, I knew that I wanted to begin my career in tech sales.

I was highly motivated by the sales environment's fast pace, emphasis on communication, and broad reach across industries. As an eager learner with skills in communication and persistence, I was able to achieve top results on my team. **While making 80 outbound calls per day, I averaged about 1.5 meetings per day - 18% of which resulted in closed sales.**

Why LinkedIn?

While speaking with LinkedIn employees and researching the company, I constantly found myself appreciating everything I was learning.

LinkedIn is highly successful in its core vision - to create greater economic opportunities for everyone in the world. **As a person who is passionate about interpersonal connections and effective communication, I feel truly connected with LinkedIn and the global impact that it continues to create.**

I am looking forward to engaging with you!

Sincerely,
Joe Smith

This is one of many types of cover letter examples. Consult your school's career center resources for more information.

"Always do more than is required as an investment in your future."

Sean O'Keefe

"Taking an active role in connecting with professionals took me from a community college student to a graduate of a four-year university with almost two years of work experience in financial services by the time I graduated. By leveraging the Career Launch methodology, **I was able to land multiple investment banking, wealth management, and hedge fund internships throughout college as well as a full-time job for after graduation.**"

Camron T.
Class of 2019

Productivity Tips & Being Mentally Strong

4 Productivity Secrets to Get More Done

As a student, your attention gets pulled in many directions: homework and exams for your classes, part-time jobs, meetings for student organizations, applying to jobs or internships, making new friends, exercise, family, sleep… the list goes on.

On top of that, staying focused is hard. We live in a golden age of distractions, and every website and device seems to be conspiring to hook us away from the projects and tasks that matter the most.

We all have the same 24 hours in a day, but some students understand certain productivity secrets that allow them to get more done in less time. When you implement these four tips, you will have more free time to spend the way you want.

1. Understand the Fundamental Productivity Equation

 Work accomplished = Time spent x Intensity of focus

What you get done isn't just about *how much* time you spend, it's about *how intensely* you are focused on the task you are doing. Author Cal Newport coined the term "pseudo-work" to describe when someone is "working," but is spending so much time checking their phone, switching tasks, and chatting with friends that they don't get much done. If you've ever tried to do homework while checking social media and texting, you know what pseudo-work feels like.

This equation means that you can accomplish more in less time if you work more intensely. You should still take frequent breaks, but during "work" time, you should be fully present and engaged in the task you are doing.

One time management technique called "Pomodoro Technique" involves short bursts of 25 minutes of focus followed by a 5-minute break. You might also decide to work for 50 minutes then taking a 10-minute break. Experiment to find what works best for you.

Productivity Tips

2. Turn Off Notifications

Notifications are engineered to hijack your brain. Every time you see a pop-up, feel a buzz, or hear a beep from your phone, your brain releases a chemical called dopamine which gives you a brief feeling of happiness. Unfortunately, this makes notifications addicting, often leading to anxiety, loneliness, and distraction.

Willpower is overrated when it comes to avoiding distractions. It is really difficult not to look at a buzzing phone or an enticing TV show. You don't need more willpower, you just need to control your environment.

The solution is to turn off all notifications during times you are working by putting your phone in airplane mode. If you implement this habit for just 2-4 hours throughout each day, you will see a massive increase in your productivity.

Even when you aren't doing intense work, it's a good idea to only use notifications for your calendar. You'll find yourself checking your phone less often, giving you more time to devote to people and projects that matter to you.

Your Productivity Checklist

1. Work for short, intense bursts
2. Turn off notifications
3. Create a schedule for every day
4. Do the most important or difficult task first

3. Create a Schedule for Every Day

The best way to accomplish what you want is to use your calendar or planner to make a schedule for every day. Your goal isn't to be perfect—some tasks will take longer than planned and unexpected things will pop up. However, the act of planning your day will give you a structure for success. You will never need to ask, "what should I be working on now?" You can just put your head down and follow the plan.

Let's run through an example. You wake up Tuesday at 7:30 a.m. and want to plan your day. You have work in the morning, a class in the afternoon, and a group meeting from 4:15-5:15 p.m. You also have 50 pages to read for your class, two small homework assignments, a history test in two days to study for, and you want to spend 30 minutes contacting professionals for career conversations. The best way to accomplish all these goals is to assign them into time blocks in your calendar or planner.

Here's what your schedule might look like:

Time	Task
7:30 am	get ready for day
8 am	study for history test
9:30 am	part-time job
12 pm	lunch break
1 pm	finish homework assignments
3 pm	history class
4:15 pm	contact professionals
5 pm	group meeting
6 pm	exercise
7 pm	dinner & relax

4. Beat Procrastination by "Eating the Frog"

What does it mean to "eat the frog"? It means that every day you **do your ONE most difficult or important task first** while still making time for all other obligations and time commitments.

Let's say it's Wednesday morning of the week before final exams. You have three small assignments due the next day which will each take about 30 minutes. You also haven't spent enough time studying for your economics exam, which you think won't be too challenging. Finally, what's stressing you out most is that you haven't started writing the big English paper due next week. What should you work on?

In this case, starting your English paper is likely the most important task, even though it isn't due right away. You should start your day by working on the essay, and work on the other assignments later.

Sometimes you have 12 things to accomplish in a day. Applying the "eat the frog" technique means that you shouldn't worry about all 12 at once. **You should start by devoting focused time to only one task that you believe is most crucial to your future success.**

▶ How will you apply these four tips to your life?

_____

_____

_____

_____

_____

_____

The 5 Habits of Mentally Strong People

You have likely thought about your physical strength, but what about your mental strength?

Becoming mentally strong, according to psychologist and author Amy Morin, means that you "manage your emotions, thoughts, and behaviors in a way that sets you up for success in life."

Mentally strong people have bad days and experience failure just like everyone else. The difference is in how they respond to these obstacles. The good news is that anyone can develop their mental strength. Here are five habits of mentally strong people that you can practice.

1. Stay grounded in your self-worth and in things you can control

It's natural to compare yourself to others. And in these days, social media makes this easier than ever. Maybe you're scrolling through Instagram and see one of your friends got an internship that you didn't, while your other friend is vacationing in Hawaii. And you take this all in while you're alone in your room, struggling to find a job or pass a class.

But social media does not determine your self-worth. Rather than focusing on what other people think of you, think about your own personal growth, what actions you can take to become the person you want to be, and how you can best support others.

2. Embrace and adapt to change

Change is often painful and disorienting. But it can also be a fun adventure.

Look for small opportunities to get out of your comfort zone, such as conducting career conversations with professionals you've never met, taking up a new creative hobby, or setting a challenging, yet realistic goal for yourself. These small steps will help you build the muscle of being resilient—or even comfortable with—change in all areas of your life.

3. Focus more on the process than on results

The Career Launch Method is intentionally designed to give you a process for action. Learning about someone's career is something you can control (if you get a conversation), but getting an internship or job is out of your control. But if you change your definition of success from getting a job to exploring careers and building relationships, you'll put yourself in a position to achieve your goals.

This applies in school as well. Rather than worrying about what grade you get on an exam, worry about how well you know the material and contribute to group projects. This doesn't mean that goals aren't valuable motivators. But by focusing on positive habits, you will build the resilience for when times are tough and set yourself up for success.

4. Learn from your mistakes and learn vicariously to prevent future mistakes

Many students avoid situations where they might make mistakes to keep failure at a safe distance. However, this habit will prevent you from learning and growing. Mistakes are an important and natural byproduct of being proactive. You should try to improve when you make mistakes rather than try to avoid them.

You should also do your best to learn from the mistakes of others through your personal relationships as well as media like books, videos, and podcasts. Take advantage of the many life lessons that have been learned and shared by others.

5. Offer support and gratitude to others

There's a quote I love by Zig Ziglar that says, "You can have everything in life you want, if you will just help other people get what they want."

Adding value to other people's lives—in school, work, and your personal life—is both the right thing to do and the best way to achieve your goals. Success isn't achieved alone, and neither is happiness. By trying to actively serve others, you will build positive relationships that will benefit you for the rest of your life.

Growth Mindset Quotes

Some will, some won't, so what

You've got nothing to lose and lots to gain

It's a numbers game. Not everyone will say yes, and that's okay!

"While one person hesitates because they feel inferior, the other is busy making mistakes and becoming superior."
-Henry C. Link

"You have to take advantage of an opportunity of a lifetime in the lifetime of the opportunity. "
- Eric Thomas